"F*#! LOW DAYS"
AND OTHER SENTIMENTS

By Women Who Dominate Depression and Anxiety

**"F*#! LOW DAYS!"
AND OTHER SENTIMENTS**

Published by
Queen Ex Literature and Pear Shaped Press

Copyright © 2021 by Pear Shaped Press and Queen Ex Literature. All rights reserved.

This book or any portion thereof may not be reproduced or used in any manner whatsoever without the express written permission of the publisher except for the use of brief quotations in a book review. For information on getting permission for reprints and excerpts, contact: pearshapedpress@gmail.com

Printed in the United States of America
First Printing, 2021
ISBN 978-1-7360522-2-8

Queen Ex Literature
www.QueenExLit.com
2711 North Sepulveda Boulevard, Suite 1021
Manhattan Beach, CA 90266

Pear Shaped Press
12225 NW Oxford St
Camas, WA 98607
http://www.pearshapedpress.com

"F*#! LOW DAYS"

AND OTHER SENTIMENTS

By Women Who Dominate Depression and Anxiety

COMPILED BY QUEEN EX LITERATURE AND PEAR SHAPED PRESS

DEAR QUEEN, FOCUS...

DISCLAIMERS

Information in this book is NOT intended as medical advice, or for use as diagnosis or treatment of a health problem, or as a substitute for consulting a licensed medical professional. The contents and information in this book are for inspirational use only and are not intended to be a substitute for professional medical advice, diagnosis, or treatment. Always seek the advice of your physician or other qualified health providers for medical conditions. Never disregard professional medical advice or delay in seeking it because of something you read in this book or any resource.

The authors and publishers have left out names and identifying details to protect the privacy of individuals. The authors may have tried to recreate events, locales, and/or conversations from the authors' memory of them. In order to maintain privacy, the authors and publisher have in some instances left out the name and identifying details of individuals. Although the authors and publisher have made every effort to make sure all information is correct at press time, the authors and publisher do not assume and hereby disclaim any liability to any party for any loss, damage, disruptions caused by stories with this book, whether such information is a result of errors or emission, accident, slander or other cause.

A LETTER FROM THE EDITORS

Dear reader,

Thank you so much for picking up this book! The original concept for "Fuck Low Days!" and Other Sentiments began as a place for women to express their particular experiences with being victorious over struggles with mental health. As poets and writers, we have all seen a lot of writing about the depths that our mental illnesses can take us to, and there is certainly value in expressing and witnessing those lows. However, the only alternative we typically found was overt positivity, which can sometimes be helpful but often borders or fully crosses over into patronizing.

So, we set out to create a space for women to talk about the in-between, for the moments when we're fighting, tired, but hopeful. Our contributors showed up to this project with a level of honesty, vulnerability, and care we could not have imagined. Some of their writing will offer you encouragement on the days when you need a little pick me up, and some of their pieces will sit down on the floor next to you and say "Yep, this sucks. We're going to get through it, but right now, it sucks."

Recovering, healing, and bouncing back are all messy, nonlinear processes. This is not a self-help book or a book that seeks to rush you past the hard things in life. Fuck Low Days and Other Sentiments is a place for conversation, where women of all ages, experiences, and walks of life have come together to be in a community with you. Their stories speak to each other as peers, mentors, and friends. We hope that this book will become a friend to you the way it has to us.

We are so thankful to our contributors for making this project what it is. You can find their names listed in the back of the book. We are also so grateful for our amazing models, whose stunning photos fill this book and add strength, joy, and encouragement to every page.

No matter where you are in your mental health journey, we hope this book speaks to you.

All our best,

Brytney, Christina, Megan, and Stephanie

Special Thanks to
Danielle Cassias, Copy Editor

INTRODUCTION

LOW DAYS SUCK.

You're not alone. There are so many women out there who know what a constant battle with mental health feels like. Thanks to the media, even those who don't experience depression or anxiety know what it could look like to be overtly battling such darkness. What they don't see are those who are functioning with these issues.

Women who deal with "low days" don't always wear their hair in disarray or turn to drugs and alcohol. They don't always cry all the time or become anti-social. Mental health issues can be personified in that well-to-do businesswoman or that happy-go-lucky cashier. Some are faking it to make it through the day. Others wear their heart on their sleeve and could go into an explosion of emotions in a heartbeat. Some have the hardest time putting their feet on the floor in the morning because their dream life is easier to deal with than everyday realities. We've been there, but most importantly, we have been through it and know what the other side looks like.

So, who are these vibrations, these events, or experiences to tell YOU how to be or who to be? What audacity do these spirits have that they feel so bold as to test your resolve to be happy? How dare depression and anxiety shroud your joy with worry or self-doubt? Don't you know who you are? This book is designed to help you remind those low moments that they are temporary and not made to last. "Fuck Low Days!" and Other Sentiments is a bright, feel-good photobook with personal essays, poetry, and stories from women who are conquerors over the same things you may be going through. They have all come together to support YOU. Every face you see and every word you read has been with YOU and your VICTORY in mind.

Whenever a low day creeps up and you find yourself feeling far from high frequencies, pick up this book and flip to a random page. Read an entry. Stare at your favorite photo. Let the bright colors and faces arrest your melancholy, chokehold your fears into submission, and make room for a smile. For a quick reminder, take in our 1-minute letters to you. "Dear Queen..." pages have mantras to help refresh self-perception and awareness.

We asked our community of women how they would describe their victory over low days and how they would encourage readers to push. There is no set blueprint for escaping suicidal thoughts, anxiety, or depression. These things tend to attack periodically - and without much warning - but this book is the perfect pick-me-up that invites you to look at low days and boldly give them the finger.

DEAR QUEEN,

You have **OVERCOME** moments that you thought would last forever. Don't allow whatever obstacles that are in front of you **CURRENTLY** stop you from **PROGRESSING FURTHER.**

I GOT OUT OF BED TODAY.
YEEEESSSSS!!!!!

ACHIEVEMENT NUMBER ONE, UNLOCKED. Now that the hardest part is over, it's time for a pat on the back, a breath of fresh air, a twirl under the sun, or maybe even a morning jam that moves your tush into the next part of your day. When praying and hoping for brighter days, one must expect opportunities in the day for its light to shine. They say depression is worry about the past and anxiety is worry about the future, so living in the present is key. I start by relishing the small, enjoyable events of the day (from morning poops to karaoke in the car) and then letting my gratitude expand for those moments. Focusing on these is often a cure-all that all started with getting out of bed. Kudos!

QUEEN BEE
OF MY BRAIN!!!!!

Six years ago, my world fell apart and at that same time, I started hearing voices.

They talk to me all the time. I wake up. Voices. I go to the bathroom. Voices. I eat. Still voices. All day long voices, voices, voices. Medicine doesn't take them away, nor does pretending they aren't there. I can choose to listen to them, ignore them, or talk to them, but still they mumble on and on.

I lost my career because of them. It's true and I resent them for it. I try daily to forgive both them and me, but I may spend the rest of my life on disability.

Very few of my friends understood what I was going through. I lost most of them. I don't blame them. How could they understand? I don't understand. In fact, there was a time I was so mad about the voices that I didn't like myself. I would have unfriended me if I could.

But I've had a lot of years to make peace with my situation and make friends with the voices in my head.

I almost can't imagine life without them. We've learned how to be quiet on occasion so it's not always Grand Central Station in my mind. They learned not to bother me when driving, or most of the time in public. It is more manageable these days. If this is happening to you, there is hope.

The first thing I had to learn was that they were not me. Just because they say something horrible, doesn't mean I think that same thing. I am me, and I am not responsible for what they say.

The second thing I had to learn was not to trust them. They stopped pulling stunts like telling me my mother had fallen when I stopped believing them.

The third thing was that it is ok to be disabled. This one is hard. But as soon as I could accept my situation, I didn't have the expectation that they would go away, or the yo-yo of emotion hoping they would leave, only to be disappointed they are still here.

Lastly, I am the master of mind, king of the hill, and ruler of the roost. Don't give away your power. I am the queen bee of my own brain. They may drone on, but I'm in charge.

If this has happened to you, I assure you it gets better. I can't promise you it will go away, though I hear for some people it does. But, if you are like me, you get used to the noise. You are able to think and drown them out when necessary. Life rebuilds with better friends and new hobbies. It is a burden I didn't ask for, but I try to find new ways to improve my life daily. Believe it or not, these days, the voices do too.

DEAR QUEEN,

LIFE CAN BE HELL;
learn to love fire.

MS. NEGATIVITY WILL STOP AT <u>NOTHING</u> TO STOMP OUT YOUR SPIRIT.

HOLD YOUR HEAD HIGH AND TELL THAT BITCH
you love a challenge!

GODDESS WITHIN ME

Just because I cry and show the emotions hidden buried deep inside, boiling over like a hot kettle atop a fiery heat, does NOT mean I am weak. I am a woman— feminine and divine. With the sway of my hips I demand the attention of others as I walk into the room. I exude a fiery passion that's shown in the way I use my walk and how strong my voice is. Unshaken and unafraid. Just because I'm a woman does NOT mean I am meek, though the meek will inherit the earth and everything it offers. She understands the struggles of those that identify as women, for She has dealt with the poison and backlash of those She tries to nurture and care for. I am black— made from clay of Aphrodite. The strongest Amazon that ever lived. Nubia. Twins. Sisters. Bonded by the dirt underneath our feet is where we get our strength. Chains broken. Blessed by the water given by Yemaya. Able to be connected to the elements enough to create tsunamis of power. Storm. Carrying a sword with rings, guarding the spirit that lays within me from any attack. Ashanti. Abundant enough to supply the ones that need the most vital thing in life. Mujaji. Goddess I am. Goddess you are. Twins. Bonded with love, bravery, and trust. We are one. A mirror with two sides. A reflection showing inside, showing a clear side to see through. Women are powerful, never to be underestimated or ignored.

MY ANXIOUS SELF

My anxious self has weathered many storms.
I am pushed and pulled,
I am tossed about,
I am covered in debris of self-loathing.

My anxious self has stood in downpours.
I am drenched with tears,
I am covered in sweat,
I am left to drown in a pool of others' expectations.

My anxious self can feel the lightning near.
I am on the verge,
I can feel the magnetic charge,
I am left to burn for the ticks of my own imperfections.

My anxious self cannot stand anymore.
I am covered in debris of doubts,
drowning in guilt,
and burning with rage.

I need to be more than the anxious
self-reflected in the mirror.
I need to be more than the cuts and
bruises.
I need to be more than pain and
voices.

But who am I without her?
I've never known a time without a
season of thunderous sorrow.
I've never known a time without the
maddening voices of the meek.
For I know, even if my anxious self is
not who I'd like to be,
who I want to be,
I know that after the seething storm,
I can feel the rainbows.

F*!K THIS DAY

Fuck this day that stole my friend. That brought then took her final breath, spinning it aloft to her beloved stars. Spiraling the bright planets that spoke to her, as I hope she will soon speak to me.

Fuck this day we light the Shoah candles. One for each million dead. Those for whom we stand as witness in prayer, and in memory. Resolved and pledged. Honor bound to remember.

Fuck this day when our love died. One hollow word, the first untruth. (At least the first I caught.) I closed my ear to echoes, but after you... moved in so fast. Fuck the day I ran from knowing, and fuck all the wasted years.

Fuck this day's depressing news. Fuck greedy lying thieves, and putting kids in cages. Fuck torch-lit Nazis in the streets and history's mocking bark. Fuck all that we have not yet learned. And fuck the looming dark.

Fuck this day when cancer wins. When the time for choice is past. Fuck feeble threats of Next life... and fuck each last weeping hug. Fuck this life with too few days and fuck the end of hope.

Fuck this day of so many hurts. A friend I cannot save. My mother's doubting voice. Fuck every lover now departed, and every sad no-longer dream.

Fuck this day that says Slow down. Let everyone catch up before you leap ahead. Fuck their heavy silence, and fuck me pretending to be the one they see. And fuck when even I begin to doubt the truest inner me.

Fuck this day of choices. And fuck that none of them is you. Fuck this day of ashes and all my dammed up tears.

BUT, TOO, I....

Bless this day I woke up smiling. I dreamed of us playing, laughing, smiling. Delicious with desire. Sweet and savory, gifting joy. Fulfilled then hungry. Again, again, again.

Bless this day that smells of coffee. That smiles sun through every crevice, demanding everything of me.

Bless this day of rain and books and cocoa, asking only for my cozy silence and napping by the fire.

Bless this day my body answers. No longer supple, yet still asking me to walk and dance.

Bless this day when lists were made and lists were conquered. When evening greets me satisfied by every meager triumph.

Bless this day of hopes and visions. And bless this day of simple living. Bless this day of friends and family. Adventures shared. A poem written. A bedtime story told. My two cats snuggled. The garden mulched. A life well-made, with more to come tomorrow.

Bless this day of prayers answered. Of laughter, of memories, and of desire. Bless this day of hope and healing. Bless this day I rise to greet.

DEAR QUEEN, WHEN ALL ELSE FAILS, DO YOU.

IT'S CALLED
SCHLUNKING

Schlunking is what we say each morning, my soul sister and I, in our ritual daily phone call. The proof of life we need to hear. Enough to rouse us to another day.

8:43 A.M.

> HI. YOU UP?

> YUP. GOT NOTHING TO SAY.

> WHAT TIME YOU WAKE UP?

> 3, BUT GOT BACK UNDER UNTIL 6.

> YOU SCHLUNK?

> OF COURSE.

> HAD YOUR COFFEE?

> I TRIED BUT FAILED. PURE CAFF TODAY!

> ME TOO.

> FIRST CUP. BUT STILL HAVE ZIP TO TELL YA.

> EVERY DAY FOR ME SISTER. I STILL HAVE A JOB!

We laugh together.

Schlunking is our safety zone, where germs and Nazis dare not invade. It begins when dreams escape, separating night from day. That quickening. The realization that we are tied to here, to this body, this bed, this now. When thoughts begin, asking us to welcome day. When clouds of imagery recede, allowing fear and apprehension to slip under.

Often, we recoil. Asked to leave our safe veiled havens, we burrow in, praying our warm covers will grant us pardon. We seek insulation, the not-knowing of life's harsh and gritty places. We crave the quiet dark, that holds us close and safe.

But at the edges, day knocks again.

We groan and grab our phones, those chatty friends who offer bites of consolation. Scrolling: Instagram, Facebook, perhaps some games or email. Anything to ward off the day. Carefully winding into new positions without disturbing a sleeping cat or partner. Urgently willing bladders to be still for just a little longer. Savoring the warm cocoon, as anxiety and sadness wait to lay their claim on us.

Slowly we stiffen and brace for what is coming. We test the headlines: Politico and Vox. Even clickbait. Remind ourselves that yesterday has always birthed today, and we are still here, alive and safe, at least for now.

Schlunking comforts with denial. No reasons to get up. Cannot remember why we should leave the cozy womb. Or when we do, decline.

She asks me, "What's your today? I promised Edel I would take her to the store. Plus Meals on Wheels takes longer since Elena died of Covid. Then baking bread with Ed to deliver to the food pantry. He wants to help build mini-houses for the camp along the river. You?"

"After work I'm gonna tutor math to my friend's dyslexic daughter. Then bringing all the masks I sewed over to the clinic. Never enough time. The lists keep growing."

"I'm ready for a nap."

We laugh in unison. Living in this new world of ours, as distant a planet as Hollywood ever conjured. When will it end? What if it doesn't? A world of questions we rarely dare to ask.

Each day we wrestle with new confusing boundaries, or sometimes none at all. Each day we rise and do our best. One step, one word, one prayer, each upon the next. With evening to call us home, until daybreak's harsh tomorrow. But in our schlunking we can pretend, for even just an hour, that everything will be okay. At least until we rise to greet the new uncertain day.

DEAR QUEEN,
ALL THAT YOU DO,
DO WITH YOUR MIGHT,
FOR THINGS DONE
HALF ARE NEVER
DONE RIGHT.

**THREE DEEP BREATHS
(YOU'VE GOT THIS....)**

In high school I invented a magic spell.

"THREE DEEP BREATHS AND YOU'LL BE OK."

It started as something unconscious. I had read online somewhere that as long as you can take three deep breaths, you'll be able to focus. It was science, a trick to fool my nervous system into thinking that danger had passed. A whispered promise when I felt like I was unraveling after a panic attack. But it became magic the day my friend broke up with her partner of two years. She needed to see her ex after school one last time-- to explain why, and to say goodbye.

She desperately tried to stop the tears rolling down her cheeks. In a spur-of-the-moment decision, I pulled her aside.

"BREATHE IN. BREATHE OUT. THREE DEEP BREATHS AND YOU'LL BE OKAY."

"I'm going to teach you a magic trick," I said, We breathed together, and I repeated the words with each breath. By the time we pulled apart, the tears had stopped. It was like magic. A magic spell for drying tears.

Let's talk about the stuff we're not supposed to:

"the perfect body".....

PLAYING THE PERFECT HOT GIRL

I have large breasts and a pretty face. Growing up and being perceived as hyper-feminine, I felt like I owed it to the world to play the role of "hot girl." My identity in the public eye was largely a performance of femininity and desire. You know the tropes. I cleaned up after the parties to prove I was wifey material. I dumbed myself down in conversation, acted ditsy, and let men sexualize me in ways I would never let slide now. I remember the feeling of coming home and putting down the performance. It's like the feeling of taking off your bra and make-up, but instead of physical relief, it was psychological. At home, I could be goofy and nerdy and as gender fluid as I felt inside.

I wanted so badly to be perceived how I felt, but at that impressionable age, my desire to fit into society's image of me was strong. Thank you, advertising, film, and 1,000 years of gender stereotypes! The disconnect between my external experience of performing perfect hot girl, and my internal experience as a gender-fluid weirdo created a sort of identity dysmorphia.

As I crept into my early 20's I naturally started to reject the performance of hyper-femininity because of this identity dysmorphia. But instead of coming to peace with my naturally curvy body, I starved myself to get rid of my breasts and hips and I cut off my hair. I didn't want to be "sexy" or "womanly," I wanted to look like a writer. I felt that if I wanted my gender fluidity to be valid in the eyes of my peers, I had to look less like everyone else deemed as feminine.

Acceptance of the performance of femininity turned to rejection of the performance. Still, both existences solidified the place of the performance in my life by acknowledging it. As I lost more weight, I did not feel connected to my inner self, I felt farther away from it. I'm happy to say that since then, I have gotten past the worst of my eating disorder. I've also done the work to reflect on my experiences and just how I got to the place I did. I realized I've always been fluid. I have always believed that the soul is a genderless being. As a writer, I am more concerned with soul than anything else.

As a young girl, no one showed me how to live this truth because fluidity is dangerous to a society which relies on the imperial practice of labeling so we can understand and control. I wish I could go back and hug little Lee. I want every child to know:

NO LABEL COULD EVER ARTICULATE THE VASTNESS OF YOUR GLORIOUS BEING.

The work that I do with this knowledge does not actually require any work. Now, my fluidity is defined by my practice of just being. I just am, and being is effortless. I love and make love to whoever, emit whatever energy I'm feeling, masculine or femme. I don't care if it doesn't make sense, or can't be articulated. I don't think it should be.

That's not to say that my days are filled with spotless self love. I still have those feelings about my breasts and my body. I still sometimes look at it and wish that I could shrink. But when I go into that place of just being, where I know nothing can be named, I acknowledge and accept those negative emotions with grace and let them pass through me. I become aware of the thought and in doing so put space between me and it.

When my mind says, "I hate myself and my body," the awareness of that thought responds, "Ok, so? I am still here."

Doing this has enriched my definition of self-love in such intense ways. Now, when I feel joy for my body, it's the feeling of aliveness that radiates from it. It's not the joy of fitting into America's racist beauty standards, but of being a conscious, loving human.

My gender fluidity is not about validation or understanding myself in terms of thought or social concepts. It's just about being my glorious godly self while I do the work to unlearn the binaries of "man and woman," "femme and masc," "ugly and desirable," that this horrible country has drilled into our malleable and innocent brains. Our brains love us in the end. Every cell in your body loves you. Forgive yourself for anything you may have done.

Now, when men underestimate me, I'll just laugh as I take their job! When men catcall me, I'll be annoyed, but I won't blame my body. I'll let it pass. I'll keep my peace.

MY PSORIATIC ARTHRITIS GIVES THE TOAST
AT MY 34TH BIRTHDAY PARTY

To the tenderness of your lover's hands putting your
hair up and clasping your bra
on mornings when your fingers crack
like bubbles in frozen champagne,
when pain
transforms you into a statue of yourself.

>To the red dress of itchy, angry skin
>that shame shoved in the back of your
>closet, locked
>away from touch
>that you now wear like a Gucci,
>like a Prada at a premiere.

>>To the pixie cut you consented to give your tired, thinning hair
>>after avoiding your reflection in the gaze of those you love
>>for a year,
>>surrendering to the beautiful bad-ass that was hiding
>>underneath.

>>>All hail the body of now, not the one you wanted,
>>>not thin, not flexible, not athletic,
>>>not even healthy,
>>>but the body who carried you through a thousand days
>>>of "fuck! this hurts so much please kill me now."

>>>>All hail the mind of now,
>>>>who said "fuck the pain, I'm going for a run"
>>>>and settled
>>>>for a slow walk after 50 meters,
>>>>but still walked, walked, walked.

>>>>>All hail the soul of now,
>>>>>who said "fuck the pain, I still want to live!"
>>>>>Still want.
>>>>>To live.

DEAR QUEEN, WORK IT!

YOU ALREADY HAVE
THE "PERFECT" BODY

I'm not going to tell you your body's "perfect" because it's functional, it shuttles you to work and happy hour, or because it lets you have great sex or puts up with you when you smoke that occasional cigarette or overdo it on whisky.

Let's talk about the stuff we're not supposed to—that "perfect body" we've dreamt up in our heads that's a collaboration of celebrities, the girl we thought was beautiful in sixth grade, the girl our first crush dated instead of us, and all too often the woman we'll never be, no matter how many restrictions, workouts, and cosmetic procedures we sign up for. No matter the subject, we want what we can't have.

I was 35 years old when I learned I had the perfect body. After spending three decades hating almost every part of my body, abusing it by putting on 100 pounds in college, nearly killing it with anorexia and exercise-induced bulimia in my early thirties, and undergoing one hell of a nine-hour surgery in a developing country just to get rid of all that saggy skin, it was three seconds after a yoga class that clued me in.

I had just finished teaching a woman in her late forties. It was her first yoga class. She was complaining that she thought her butt was too big. As someone with a notoriously flat "Indian butt" (seriously, my butt was concave even when I was obese), I've always been amazed at women who don't have to work tirelessly for what passes as a "normal butt." And yes, I hear self-loathing too, even as I write this.

I'm terrible at giving forced compliments, and I wanted to deflect her own self-deprecating statement, so I told her to be careful what she wished for. At least she wasn't doing three hours of weighted squats, lunges, various leg raises and adductor raises with ankle weights every week just to have a "regular butt."

She looked at me in total disbelief.

"BUT YOUR BODY'S PERFECT," SHE SAID.

It wasn't a shrugged-off compliment. She really meant it, and with no ulterior motive. It wasn't even to be nice—it was simply her shocked reply. To a woman I'd never met before, my body really was perfect.

I could push it aside and tell myself, "Well, she didn't see all the scars under my tank top and the crepe-like skin thanks to a lack of elasticity and severe weight swings." I could make all kinds of excuses for why she was wrong. But she wasn't wrong. Not for her—and, maybe one day, not for me either.

Here's the truth: There are people, probably a lot of people, who would truly think your body is perfect just the way it is if they saw you. But they won't tell you that. Why? Because it seems weird, they don't want to come off as creepy, and it's just not something you say to a stranger or, sadly, to a friend.

We're all supposed to love our bodies, and we're supposed to be focusing on what really matters. When we do compliment others we're supposed to say "of course they're perfect," even when it doesn't sound genuine, but the fact remains that there are lots of incredible people out there who would say that, to them, your body is perfect.

Now, isn't that something to think about the next time that scared voice in your head pipes up? Or just when you happen to catch your reflection? So many people think your body is just so amazingly perfect, and you can join them in this consensus any time you choose—because this, it is a choice. Self-love is a choice.

DEAR QUEEN,

IT'S OKAY TO BE A B*@!H SOMETIMES.

DEAR SELF...

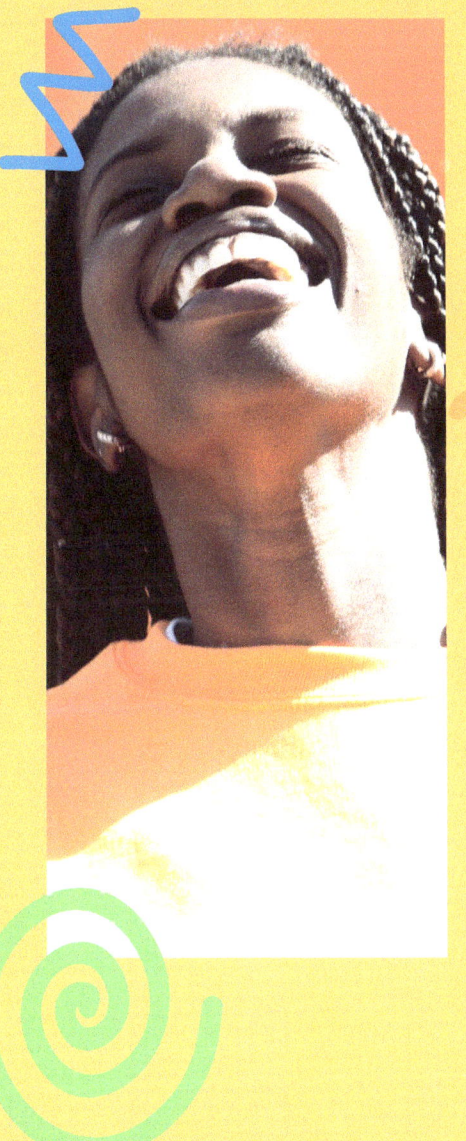

I regret every minute, of every second, of every day I spent hating you. Others convinced me that you were a monster. Now I know that you have never been anything but human. Painfully, beautifully, human. They will try to tell you that your kindness makes you weak. That the way you love will do nothing but destroy you. Whatever you do, don't listen to them. They're wrong. Your strength comes from your kindness, not in spite of it. Your capacity for love is a blessing, and while it may cause pain, it will also lead you to lifelong friends. I'm sorry that I can't get back all the time I wasted treating you like the enemy, but I promise you that from now until our death I will wake up every day and love you. I will look into those eyes and love what I see within them, whether it be pain or joy. I will love every single part of you until I can feel that love vibrating in our lungs when we exhale. I know self-love is hard. I know that we will cry and say, "I hate you," just like we always have, but the difference is that now I am choosing to love you. Even when I want to tear you to pieces, I choose to love you. I will love you because, at the end of the day, this love is all that we have.

DEAR QUEEN,

SOMETIMES YOU'RE A PAIN, BUT THERE'S NO ONE ELSE I'D RATHER SPEND EVERY WAKING SECOND WITH.

NO MATTER HOW BROKEN, **YOUR BODY IS ALWAYS A MIRACLE,** AND THERE IS NO TELLING HOW MANY **WONDERS** MAY BE BESTOWED UPON YOUR LIFE AS LONG AS YOU **KEEP PAYING ATTENTION.**

IT IS TOO LATE FOR ME TO BE YOUNG AND UNASHAMED

I spent my beautiful days believing I wasn't. Took the magazine as a mirror in which I was badly reflected. Hid my curves under black and volume. Layered products over my face to smooth out what was still unlined. Let dislike of my pale skin mar my time in the sun.

It should have just been working parts. After all, the journey is the point and not the vehicle. My car drives just as well for all its dents and scratches. There is no moral failing in needing to fix brakes or replace worn tires.

But my mind, that busybody who thinks it must know best, chose to interfere. It told me my fat was a weakness, my shape unlovable, my plainness unbearable. It hid from me, others' unhappiness. Insisted their beauty was all natural, kept their secrets of pills and purges, refused to look into their eyes, also puffed from crying.

Changing this took an out-of-body experience, seeing myself through somebody else's mind. Hearing the harsh words that I speak to myself when there is no reason. Understanding that to look like someone else would be to take away what makes me.

At first, I thought about taking out a restraining order out on my mind. I have found, though, that the best thing is to work patiently with her and help her to be less judgemental about me. Give her encouragement, but also tell her to shut up when it's needed.

Together we look forward to being old, to being truly unashamed.

HER ESCAPE: FEEL 'N' HEAL

They said Her dark skin needs to be bleached.
Her natural face, needs some makeup.
Her slim body, needs more calories.
Her height, needs to be on heels.
Her voice, too irritating, should be silenced.

To feel love, She should be with a ready-made man.
Her results should display only A's.
At 22, a graduate She should be.
At 24, a wife and a mother, She has to be.

'Crack!' She heard, when She wasn't good enough
trying to be perfect, staying in an abusive relationship.
Too tiny She felt, and stepped into a box.

'Crack! Crack!' She heard, when they laughed at Her flaws
calling Her names, making her believe She didn't deserve kindness.
Too strong, She tried to smile at every insult She got.

'Crack! Crack!!!' She heard, trying to stay in her box
made from fear, insecurities, and the negativities She was fed.
Hurting, She vowed never to feel again, for feelings had caused Her nothing but pain.

CRACK! CRACK!!!' She heard the sound, louder this time.
threatening to shatter Her ear drums.
She listened, and realized it was coming from within.
It was Her heart breaking by being caged in a toxic box.

She reached out to her heart,
picked up its pieces, assembled them all.
Silencing their judgmental voices and those of Her head, She said
"My grades don't imply how successful I am.
My physical appearance doesn't signify how beautiful I am.

Choosing and loving myself, over anyone else, doesn't indicate I'm selfish
Being happy, not caring about anything else doesn't make me heartless."

"Lub! Dub! Lub! Dub!!" She heard the sound of something she never knew existed,
Her heart was beating for the first time in years.
When She stared at her reflection, She smiled,
for through the years, She'd aged.

Wasn't as pretty as She used to be but, She felt more beautiful than She'd ever been.

She stepped out of the box to continue Her journey,
for She'd finally found Herself,
knowing that success, beauty, love, and happiness can only be defined by Her.
Her scars and flaws are what make Her story real,
for perfection is fake and never attainable,
so She wore Her invisible wings.
With them, She'll feel, She'll heal...

AND SHE'LL BE FREE.

DEAR QUEEN,

NOT GETTING PREGNANT DOESN'T MEAN YOU ARE LESS OF A WOMAN.

My Dear Child,

LETTER TO MY UNBORN CHILD

Someday soon, I will meet you and you will meet me. You will be a little stranger, a person that I will eventually get to know every single detail about, know every single life moment. I will be with you the moment your life begins. There will be no history I don't know.

Unfortunately for you, there is a lot of my life that you will never know. I've lived 32 years now, 32 years of experience and life lessons and mistakes and adventures, 32 years of love that was lost forever, love lost temporarily, a heart that was broken and mended more times than I could possibly count. All that time has made me who I am today, a person who will no doubt continue to grow and change, just as you will, but who is also shaped quite permanently.

Then again, you know a lot about me already, I imagine. You may know the sound of my voice. You may even know the feel of my touch as I gently caress the outside of my stomach where you are comfortably tucked inside. You know my unquenchable desire for dairy. You know I like to take walks, during which you inevitably are lulled to sleep. You probably know that I have uncontainable road rage, and for that, I apologize for the harsh tones and naughty words you may already be familiar with.

You must know, too, how much I love your father. You hear me tell him so many times a day how I love him, and you hear him tell me. You can probably hear my heart skip a beat when he kisses my face or looks at me lovingly. Perhaps you know his touch from mine. I know exactly where to find you in my tummy, but he has to search around a little bit, his strong hands providing a firmer grasp than I have, trying in vain to feel your movements. And when you do appease him, which isn't always, he can't help but laugh out loud, amazed by this little person we have created together.

There are a small number of good men in the world, but your father is one of them. I know he will treat you well, love you unconditionally like he loves me, and show you what great things you deserve in life, just as I will. I worry a bit about the life you have in front of you; it is predestined to be difficult and frustrating based on your sex alone. And I know that's not fair. You will have to fight for things you shouldn't have to fight for. You will have to demand respect and equality, and even then, some still won't give it to you.

But your father is strong. And I am strong. And we will teach you how to be strong, too, because you deserve everything the world has to offer and more. And I hope you take advantage of all of it. I hope you try a myriad of activities. I hope you visit countless new places. I hope you never stop learning about the world and about yourself.

At times, this will feel scary. And if you are afraid, that's okay. But try not to let fear stop you from new experiences. All experiences are valuable, even the ones that turn out to be failures. I have experienced much failure in my life, but looking back on it now, it doesn't feel like failure, because it has led me to where I am today, and I wouldn't want to be anywhere else. The only place I want to be is here with you and your father, forever and always.

Love,
Mommy

I WANT MY MOMMY

I remember enjoying the feeling of my hair being brushed while I sat and watched Sailor Moon on the TV carelessly passing her the colors of the day out of my pumpkin-themed barrette bucket. I can still feel her warm hand in mine as we walked those long walks to the Check Cashing place so she could stand in line for food stamps, yelling at my older brother not to walk too far ahead of us. Oh! The best was sitting in the space between her bent legs as she lay on the couch watching afternoon stories, my tired hand lovingly rubbing her leg as requested, and the once in a lifetime childhood feeling of safety and love.

"Mommy..."

I would cry when I felt pain, speaking the magic spell of her name knowing that the discomfort I had would go away as soon as those words were spoken with conviction. Well, I wanted to be just like her, and no one else could influence how I saw her as a person. Who could fathom I would have a world that my mommy wasn't going to be a part of? Who could predict in these childhood dreams that the story would lend in the tragedy of finding out she was human?

The cups were just cups to me and had I understood that what was inside was slowly and painfully taking her away from my future, I would have knocked over the cups she often placed on the floor on purpose instead of on accident.

I remember enjoying the feeling of my hair being brushed while I sat and watched Sailor Moon on the TV carelessly passing her the colors of the day out of my pumpkin-themed barrette bucket. I can still feel her warm hand in mine as we walked those long walks to the Check Cashing place so she could stand in line for food stamps, yelling at my older brother not to walk too far ahead of us. Oh! The best was sitting in the space between her bent legs as she lay on the couch watching afternoon stories my tired hand lovingly rubbing her leg as requested, and the once in a lifetime childhood feeling of safety and love.

From childhood to adulthood, I made it my life's mission to prove to her that she was not a bad mom, and I would prove it to anyone who said otherwise. Tossing out my own emotions and issues away into endless diaries so I could be empty enough to take the pain from her when she got home from her second job. Anticipating the tired and hurt that came with hearing her car pull up in the driveway. Changing my sleeping habits to be there for her in the middle of the night to ease against the nightmares of childhood molestation and, to my surprise, her own want for her mommy.

It wasn't until I became a mom myself that I understood the incredible burden I was given to break the cycle. It was not until I laid eyes on the face of my baby that I understood that enough was enough, without knowing what I even intended to do about it. What a position to be in for a daughter, having to choose between their child and their mother. Saying no wasn't what I knew how to do, and most importantly I didn't want to say no. I am still the little girl who believes in the beautiful healing effects of the word Mommy.

I love her. Damn it, I love her. I will always want my Mommy, and despite the heartache it requires, I refuse to let the strength of that spell die. I am finding ways to turn that want into strength in my own mothering to pass down this beautiful gift to my own child. I hold on to my golden memories of us for dear life and will probably always be holding out hope that she will return one day. I've come to terms with the fact that I don't have the same opportunity to childishly kick all the cups over, and that's ok. I'm starting to find out that in the times I really want Mommy, I can just be her.

We learn in acting classes that imitation is the highest form of flattery, and I can't think of a better way to break the cycle than becoming the mommy all the women in my family tried to be.

FAREWELL

We've all had fair-weather friends.
I've had my fair share.
Those who are happy to soak up my sunshine
and bask in my rays.

But those fairweather folk fear the floods
that come raining from my eyes.
They save themselves from the
horrors of the hurricane deep within my heart.

I've had my fair share.
So you'd think I'd know better than to fall
for a fair-weather lover.

*I wrote the first draft of this poem towards the end of the worst 9 months of my life. I was terribly depressed, in a bad living situation, and had just ended a long-term romantic relationship because my partner told me I was too depressing to talk to anymore and they wouldn't provide any emotional support when I really needed it. It was absolutely crushing, but my situation changed about a month later, and the weather cleared up for me. I managed to move on from that place, mentally and physically.

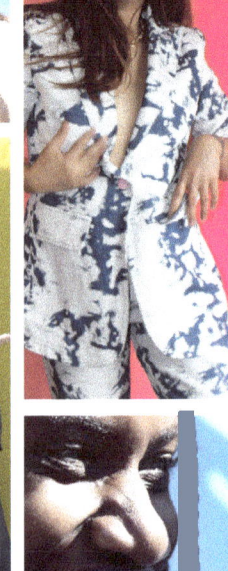
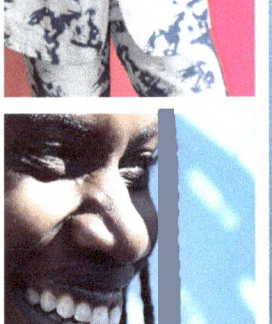

CONQUERING ANXIETY
(BECAUSE YOU CAN)

Conquering anxiety is interesting because I wonder if it's something that can truly be conquered, or if it's something we just learn to manage with the tools we've learned along the way. What triggers my anxiety is the unknown. This may sound simple, but for someone who is afraid of failure and afraid of not becoming the success envisioned in their head, it's a crippling feeling.

My anxiety began taking over me when I was 24, a few months before turning 25. Simply put, I had a quarter-life crisis. I'm obviously thankful for life, but the idea of getting older and still being in the same position (not having a significant other, not having a family of my own, feeling stagnant in my career) was something that continuously put me into a panic. Eventually, it led me into deep depression.

My family did all they could to support me, but as time continued they exhausted all they could do. The tools my therapist gave me brought me hope. That didn't take away the pain I was feeling, but day by day I felt myself become stronger. One of the things I learned was to speak back, out loud, to the negative thoughts that would enter my mind. Being able to physically hear myself pour words of life into myself was one of the main ways I was able to continue on.

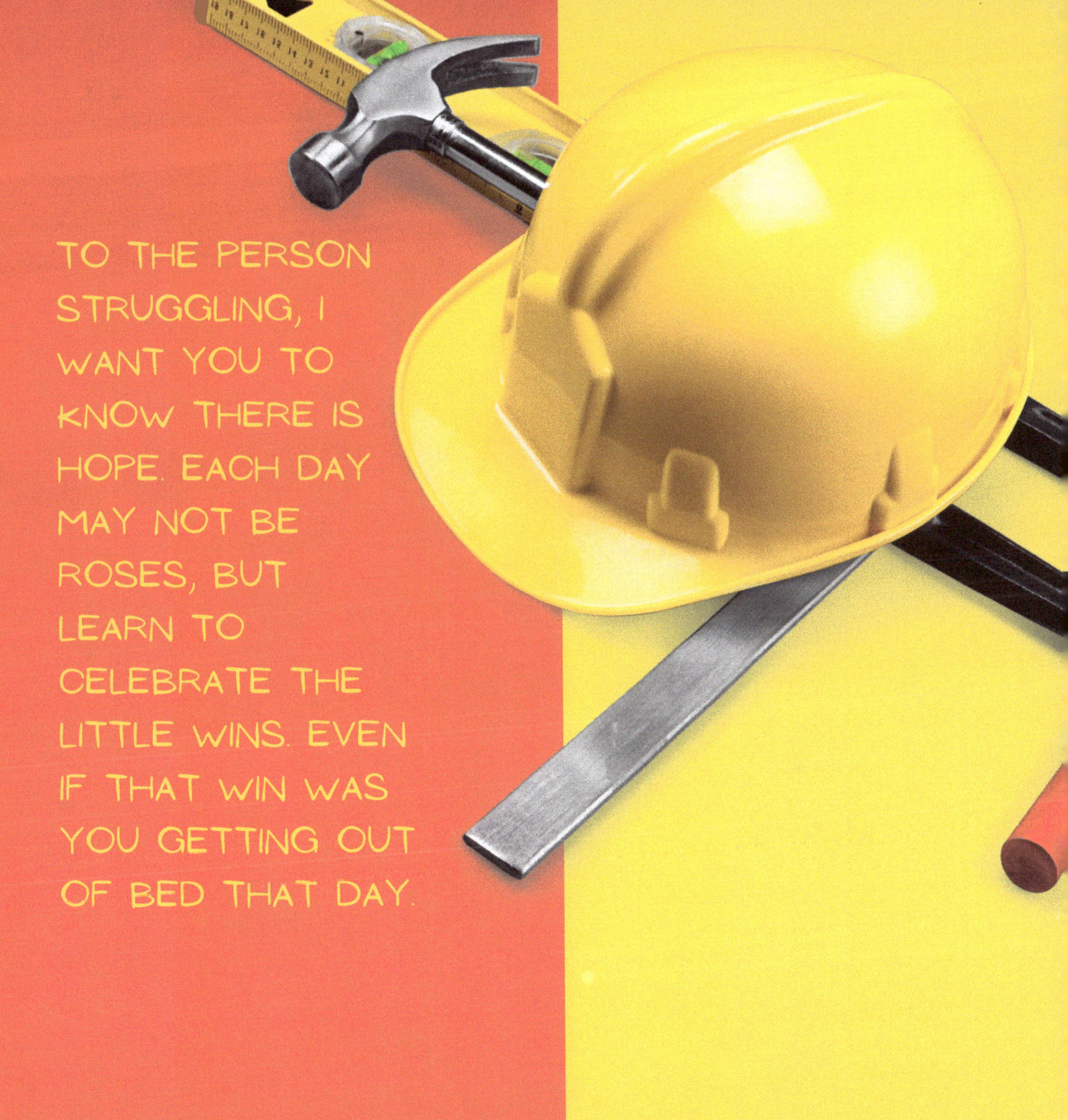

TO THE PERSON STRUGGLING, I WANT YOU TO KNOW THERE IS HOPE. EACH DAY MAY NOT BE ROSES, BUT LEARN TO CELEBRATE THE LITTLE WINS. EVEN IF THAT WIN WAS YOU GETTING OUT OF BED THAT DAY.

DEAR QUEEN, SLAY, BABE.

JOURNALING THROUGH
A PANIC ATTACK

I am proud of myself
for not being on the floor
in a heap
panicking after
a job rejection.

I am proud I am writing
through tears
trying to beat
this fucking attack.

I am proud that I am
fighting // breathing // keep // going
because I am shaking,
but trying to keep
positive through this.

I am proud of the hard
fucking work I am doing
and have done.

I am proud I asked for help
that I called NAMI,
this is using my tools.

I am proud I was able to talk
to someone, calm some
of my worry, focus
on the help I am getting.

I am proud I cried
but also used what I have learned
to "right my head."

I am proud the tears
have now stopped.

I am proud that I know
I am supported, loved,
and can use a notebook
to fight demons.

I am proud of me today.

NAMI, the National Alliance on Mental Illness, is the nation's largest grassroots mental health organization dedicated to building better lives for the millions of Americans affected by mental illness. If you or someone you know is struggling, you are not alone. There are many supports, services and treatment options that may help. www.NAMI.org

DEAR QUEEN, YOU'RE ALL THAT AND A BAG OF POTATO CHIPS.

DEAR ANXIOUS BELIEVER

I had never heard of Preeclampsia. You see, no one ever mentions the other side of motherhood. In the midst of the excitement of listening to the heartbeat, baby showers, nursery decor, and the never-ending list of things to buy, soon-to-be-first-time parents seem to skip the 'conditions that can affect your pregnancy outcome,' part in their pregnancy research. And who can blame them?

I was in the fun phase of my second trimester, when maternity photo shoots would be scheduled, hospital tours were coming up, and so were the endless supply of baby shower treats. My first child would be born in a sea of pink and polka dots. I was in bliss. And then one day, I wasn't. About 26 weeks in, I was diagnosed with Preeclampsia.

At 31 weeks, I entered motherhood with a baby that needed to be life flighted to a hospital that had a neonatal intensive care unit (NICU) an hour and a half away. It would be her home for six weeks.

Those weeks blurred into each other, and I only remember the highs and lows. There were plenty of highs, including her first bath, our first kangaroo care, meeting the grandparents......

I remember when she was upgraded from an isolate to an open crib.

I remember her "take home outfit," a purple newborn sleeper that still swallowed her.

The low points still sting. Her birthweight was 3 pounds 4 ounces. I kept it all in, because who wants to see a tiny baby covered in tubes and wires? Who wants to hear about her apnea or her loss of appetite?

We were lucky. "It could have been much worse," I was told repeatedly. So, we learned to keep our failures, our tears, and our pain to ourselves, and only dish out success stories, smiles and a brave front.

See how happy we are, social media world! We got to hold our week-old baby for the first time! She's now 4 pounds. She no longer needs to be on a nasogastric (NG) tube. When she came home, I began to hide in closets and bathrooms to cry. Was all of this real or did my broken heart imagine this homecoming?

I started to journal so as not to be swept up in the emotional current of memories and grief. Because the truth is, I was still grieving. I was grieving for the birth that I wanted. I was grieving for the six weeks that I lost in the hallways of the hospital. I was grieving for her and her early start, and her potential risks in the future.

I also didn't know what to make of my state. I didn't know if what I was going through had a name. So I continued on pretending that I was calm in the middle of my storm. Later, I was given a name; a label, mind you. A doctor called it "post-traumatic stress disorder," which is common for mothers who have traumatic birth experiences.

Getting a diagnosis is like getting a label to carry. We walk around a bit, trying to find where this label fits into our life. The thing about a label, though, is that the more we carry it around to try on, the more it takes shape. It'll never fit anywhere in our lives because it wasn't supposed to be in our story.

Just as we believe this denial, it grows. Our worries about expectations, our anxieties, and our fears of the unknown feed this strange thing, and it starts to close in beneath, around, and above us, engulfing us in its darkness. We become our labels.

Preeclampsia survivor, PTSD, and, years later, another label. Postpartum depression was one I wanted to carry. It is not a label that I could wear to "try on." You don't just try on sorrow. Or rage. Or apathy. I believed that my world would right itself somehow, and I would survive another round. Not until someone pointed out that I needed help did I even acknowledge what was happening to me. I finally reached out.

I'm still not comfortable talking about postpartum depression without feeling like a failure. I failed my children at the beginning of their lives, and I will do what I can to make sure that I won't fail them later. So with all these labels that come after my name, I hold on tight to the survivor part. I survived. I survived the roughest, toughest beginnings and one day, so will you.

DEAR QUEEN,

IF YOU WANT YOUR PASSION TO MAKE A WAY FOR YOU, YOU MUST FIRST BE AWARE OF YOUR PASSION.

DEAR QUEEN, YOU'VE GOT THIS!

KEEP YOURSELF ALIVE

I did not die today, instead I made
my favorite sandwich
ate through my tears. Held tight
a sachet full of lavender
had plenty of tissues
a list of "to do's"
but no energy to give.

The television played a movie
the first scene, Freddie Mercury singing
Keep Yourself Alive.

I nod and chuckle, need a better word for trigger.
Something less stabbing
that doesn't break my heart
or shatter me again.

I just need the word for today.

I know tomorrow
will be here soon enough.

This moment knows it will pass.

Just found two reasons to laugh
got a text, a small hi -- an old friend
that pulled me off the couch
out of the blanket
out of darkness
and I love how friendships
are soul quenching.

**I ATE THE ENTIRE SANDWICH AND FEEL BETTER;
DIDN'T USE EVERY TISSUE IN THE BOX.
I'VE SEEN THIS MOVIE BEFORE…
I HAVE A LIST OF TO-DO'S.**

ALONE DOESN'T MEAN LONELY.

I LOVE ME, BOO.

Taking time to really get used to myself with no one else around was like being in a new relationship. Some things I didn't like. Some things made me laugh. Sometimes I'd just sit and smile. Other times I'd play music to drown out the sound of my own thoughts. Still, when it came down to wanting company, I tended to choose myself because I realized that I am a dope chick. Everyone else is just regular. Who wants to be around Average Janes when Awesome Annie is right here!

DEAR QUEEN,

PAY ATTENTION TO THE <u>SPIRIT</u> INSIDE YOU - NOT THE RUNNING MOUTHS AROUND YOU.

DEAR QUEEN, DON'T FALTER WHEN YOU'VE MADE A CHOICE TO **STAND;** THE MOST HIGH IS GUIDING YOUR FEET.

EVER FLEETING

The pain that is inflicted upon me is fleeting. Like a dust particle in the wind that you can see, disappearing once you look at it from a certain angle. They can try to take away my intelligence, they can try to mark my body, they can try to cut me down to a size that's suitable to them so they aren't so intimidated or insecure. They'll never take the power that's deeply rooted in my soul, planted within me by my mother and her mother, and The Mothers before me.

SAVE ME

Stop waiting, darling.
No knight is coming.
You've been crowned
with the strength of knowing
that only you
can truly save you.
So please ,
stop chasing
what's not yours to have.
Stop searching
what doesn't want to be found.
Just stop.

**PAIN DOES NOT DEFINE ME
'CAUSE I SAID SO.**

LETTING GO FEELS LIKE
HOLY WATER

Tears that I swim in become too much for me to bear.
It feels like I'm swimming against the current of my own despair.
Keep going, keep going.
My limbs become tired, my lungs are about to give up
until I do the unthinkable.
I swallow my tears.
I swallow my tears along with my fears so that
they don't overcome me
but so that I can overcome them.
I swallowed too much and my lungs burned but
I did not give up.
I swam against the current,
I swallowed my tears until there was nothing to fear,
nothing left to potentially take me off the course
I was destined to be on.
It feels strange being able to walk again after crawling and
swimming for so long.
But it feels good to be right back on path,
knowing that the setbacks were just that.

YOU ARE HERE

DEAR QUEEN,

YOU ARE

ENOUGH.

**WEAKNESS?
I THINK NOT!**

SPITE IS HOPE WITH ITS FIST UP

I'm 19 and I get into screaming matches with my father over politics. I'm 19 and I can't turn away from the abuse of undocumented immigrants at the southern border, from the military and police sapping government funding away from the BIPOC communities that need it most, or from the capitalistic system and resulting climate change that stole my optimism for a good future. I'm 19 and the nights when my immigrant parents tucked me in with stories about how they came to the United States, yearning for a better life, are littered with irony because they support a man who has robbed my generation of that same hope.

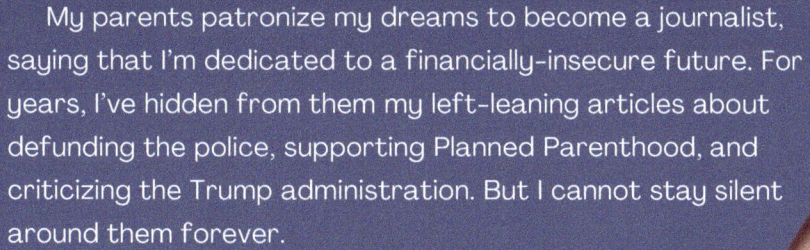

My parents patronize my dreams to become a journalist, saying that I'm dedicated to a financially-insecure future. For years, I've hidden from them my left-leaning articles about defunding the police, supporting Planned Parenthood, and criticizing the Trump administration. But I cannot stay silent around them forever.

The bell rings in my ears again. I have to keep writing. As a journalist, I cannot turn my back on people who need a voice. I will write and envision a world where the destitute have basic necessities, where black and brown people of color aren't murdered arbitrarily, and where authoritarianism is seen as a ball and chain to liberty. I have to keep writing to change the future. I am so damn tired of old men telling us, Generation Z, that it's impossible to fix everything. The phrase, "Okay, boomer," was uttered out of spite towards the condescending aggression of older generations. Spite is my desperate plea that good things can happen if we work hard enough for them.

"I WILL PROVE IT TO YOU ALL," I WHISPER WHEN MY PARENTS CAN'T HEAR ME.

DEAR QUEEN,

DON'T LOSE YOURSELF WHILE PUTTING OTHERS' NEEDS BEFORE YOUR OWN. ALWAYS HAVE AN OUTLET AND SOMETHING YOU ENJOY CLOSE BY.

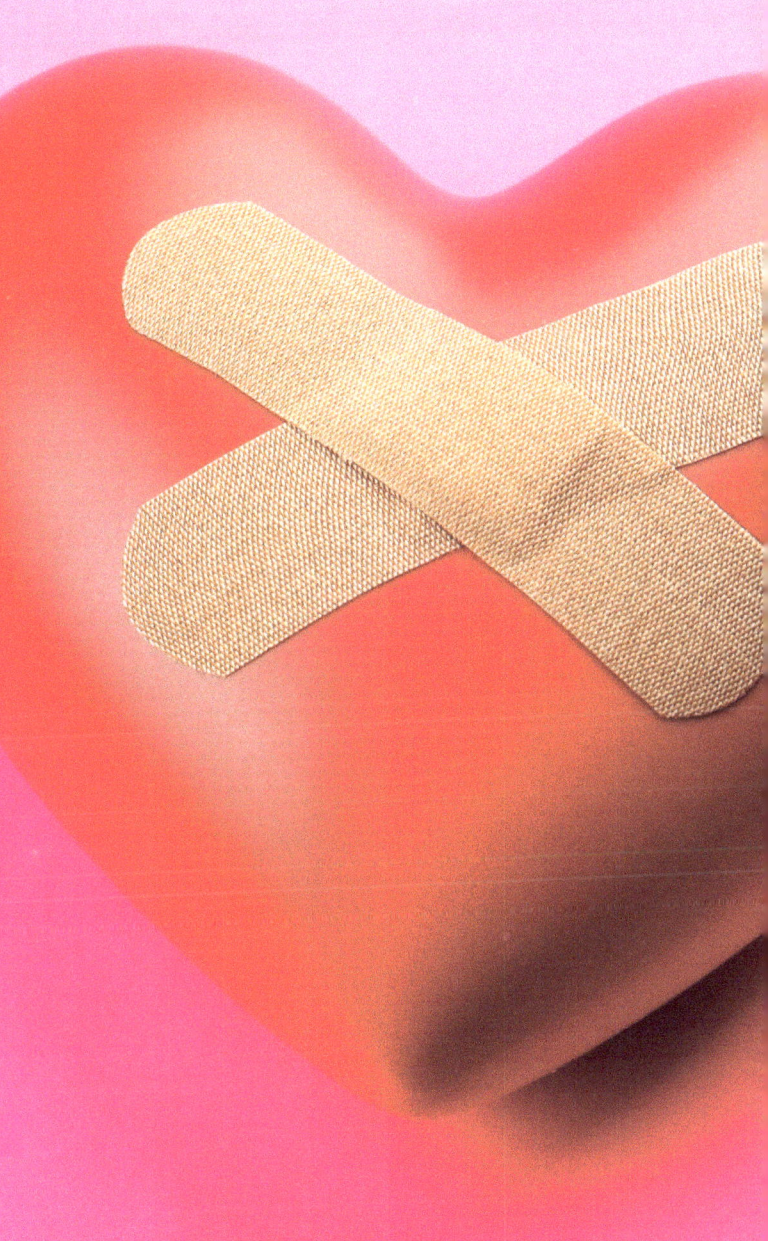

BANDAID

The first time someone tried to erase my scars, I was six. My mom brought home a goo that heralded the dent in my nose raising back to skin level, blemish-be-gone because my mom assumed I hated the scar on my nose (which I didn't) and didn't want me to look poorly cared for (which I did).

Every other week or so, my sister dragged bristles through the mats in my hair that I didn't tease away with my fingers and this, in contrast, was something I hated. Neglect and love both smell like Suave No Tears Detangling Spray, some mix of cantaloupe & discomfort; my lip pouted out just how my neighbor taught me. My hair would tangle again, so I cut it off.

My discomfort never ceased, so I began to ignore it. No one is worse at asking for help than us— us kids who were always told no when we asked for our needs and yes when we demanded our wants. Logically know that the things I would die without are needs, and everything else is a want, but that line turned to grayscale the first time depression tapped my shoulder so death could grab my ankles.

Last week, you pointed out it had been five years since she last dug her nails into my arm and crashed her fist into my stomach, and I agreed. I left the scar-be-gone goo on the bathroom counter, unused. Time doesn't heal all wounds. I do, throughout time.

Time doesn't erase them either: I choose when I heal and forgive, and can I please confess: I think her hands only hurt so badly because my skin was already bruised. I think everyone who met me as a teenager had horrible luck or some sort of awful skill. I've never wanted to get rid of my scars. These days I put bandaids over bug bites to stall my scratching fingers. They lose their hold over time, and under them, **I heal.**

DEAR QUEEN, WHEN YOU TAKE A LOSS TAKE THE LESSON THAT COMES WITH IT.

DEAR QUEEN, MAKE YOURSELF A *TOP PRIORITY* FOR ONCE.

HEY, LOVE...

I have experienced many high moments and accomplishments in my life, but as the saying goes, "what goes up MUST come down."

The ride we take as we journey through existence isn't a flat boring one! Our life is equipped with the most awesome bends, loops, highs, and dramatic lows that are found on every roller coaster ride we've been on. What we must remember is that this is our only ride, and it is one that was created to make us who we are.

I wouldn't dare eject myself on a ride at Six Flags just because I'm too afraid of what's ahead, or so beat and bent from what's behind, to say, "I quit! I give up! This is too hard and I just don't want to do it anymore!"

I'm not saying I haven't felt those very things before; what I am saying is that our FAITH has to be so much stronger than our FEARS. Our feelings of HOPE have to be so much stronger than our feelings of desperation. There is someone who needs you. There is someone who needs your story, knowledge, and advice! As women, as humans, God put us here to be that for one another, and it is at our lowest that we can begin to forge a bond with ourselves that can't be broken! You are the only person that can save you! Don't count yourself out, someone needs you!

I created a project called, "Find A Leaf". Find A Leaf is based on the life cycle of the most beautiful transformation, a butterfly! When a butterfly's life starts, it begins as a caterpillar, and when that caterpillar is ready to transform into a butterfly it finds a leaf to protect it while it's in its cocoon phase. This mantra is your protection!

When I'm speaking to young girls about hurt, pain, and loss, I encourage them to write out their own mantras. Something they can hold on to that will mentally keep them through the storm because "Life ain't easy," as my Daddy says. Then he follows it up with, "*just keep livin!*"

I sat down and wrote out all of my negative thoughts, then created power sentences that sniffed out those negative thoughts, and bold words where I place emphasis on personal interpretation. If you have a hard time creating one for yourself, try this:

> "I AM _____ (INSERT FULL NAME) AND I AM CONFIDENT IN ALL THAT I DO. I UNDERSTAND THAT GOD'S DELAY IS NOT DENIAL BECAUSE WHAT IS FOR ME IS ALREADY MINE! I'M A FIGHTER, I'M STRONG, I'M IMPERFECTLY PERFECT IN EVERY WAY. FEARLESSLY I MOVE FORWARD WITH FAITH. I CAN BE, I WILL BE, AND I AM ENOUGH!"

I hope your heart & mind can rest on the blessed assurance that these words are TRUE! They are truer than any negative thought your mind creates. You are better than any negative words someone can throw at you, even if at one point those things were true. Every day you have the choice to decide who you want to be and how you want to get there!

FIGHT!

FALSE EVIDENCE APPEARING REAL...
F*#! IT.

Once upon a time, I was afraid. My own excellence scared me. My light was so bright I feared being blinded by it. So I hid from myself, retreating to the darkness within. Mediocrity was my limit. Self-love seemed too much like selfishness, which I believed I never should be; so I loved others selflessly. Then femininity became a mere acquaintance. My grasp on who I was became loose as other people's opinions of me became a wedge between the truth. I started making decisions they wanted me to make. I lost my identity in religion, in family, in friends, and in lovers. That made me more afraid, but this time of the unknown because I knew one thing: If my light was to shine many would burn in its heat or run to the shadows. I cared too much about the others to make them suffer by my being great. I also didn't want to be alone. I had responsibilities that never were mine and so I lived in a fear disguised as compassion. I didn't succeed because the others couldn't. Success was not mine to have if they weren't with me to enjoy it. If success was to only be mine then even having that made me selfish and that was the evilest thing I could be. So, I lived in fear. 30 years of false evidence appearing real manifested into this world and now that I see the ugliness, I hate it. My disdain for what I created in my life with these false beliefs have penetrated past the bullshit narrative I had been telling myself about me.

I am not suicidal. I am not depressed. I am not sad. These things are not the real me. The real me is light, life, joy, and sun. The real me is a creator, one of the best things about God I could ever praise him for. Don't you know creatives are made closer to God's image than anyone else? Your ideas, your wit, your ingenuity, the ability to formulate something from start to finish, is the best of God's image at work within you. This is the real you, lovie.

The real you is the sunshine in your smile, the warmth in your friendship, the heart in your passion, and the humor in your laugh and even the corniest of jokes. Fear is normal to experience, and without it, we would never know courage. Without failure, we would never know the sweetness of triumph. You know fear well enough to know how to combat it. Show your courage. Count 10 Mississippi's and pull yourself up. Then count another 10 and put both feet on the floor. Yawn. Stretch. Scratch balls or whatever, then stand up. Go to the natural light outside, even if it's grey, and make yourself smile. Just smile for 60 Mississippi's and breathe deeply. This is what it feels like to conquer fear. It is a literal breath of fresh air. So when you breathe, just be like "I JUST MADE FEAR MY BITCH!." Then fist pump like a dork (or a lunatic) until you can't help but laugh or smirk cuz it felt so good to WIN.

We love you, but it is the love you have for yourself that will pull you through. Eventually, you will work yourself up to a call to friends. Then a visit. Then dinner with the dorks, I mean your family. :) (Let's face it, we're all geeks, nerds, and dorks....but the cool ones!) Most importantly, remember, dearie, that you have a support system and we got you!!!

LESS THAN -
THE PROPER EQUATION

False evidence appearing real is LESS THAN the victory you claim. Weapons formed against you are LESS THAN your faith. Bullshit is LESS THAN deserving of your attention. Perpetual sadness is LESS THAN a moment in the sun. Drama is LESS THAN necessary. Darkness is LESS THAN your light. Your life is nothing LESS THAN invaluable. Refusing to contribute to this world is LESS THAN acceptable. Your absence is far LESS THAN your value.

DEAR QUEEN,

YOU MAY FIND OTHERS ON THE SAME PATH AS YOU, BUT

YOU

GET TO CHOOSE YOUR OWN PACE.

STRONG WOMAN

I am a strong woman, but don't let that fool you.
Strength doesn't mean I am invincible, or that I gracefully go through life without pain. A strong woman is accompanied by a long history of hurt and mistakes. She hasn't always been courageous in moments she felt fear. She hasn't always been able to fight without defeat.

A strong woman takes those moments and recognizes that they are part of her journey. She understands that the burdens she wears and the baggage she carries have been difficult to endure. But she continues to fight, she continues to learn, and she continues to grow.

I am a strong woman because I allow my pain to be felt, my hurt to be healed, and my soul to tell its story.

YOUR
SUPERPOWER

If you are a star,
then you shine
in your own way
that lightens the sky.

If you are a bird,
then you sing
in your own way
that gives a different
melody.

If you are a river,
then you flow
in your own direction
that gives life to others.

There are a billion others
who might be like you,
but there's never anyone
who is exactly like you.

If you are lost,
then listen to your heart,
how uniquely it beats.
And that's your superpower.

DEAR QUEEN,

YOU ARE
BEAUTIFUL
NO MATTER WHAT.

DEAR QUEEN, IT IS TIME.

WE LOVE OUR CONTRIBUTORS, DON'T YOU?

SPECIAL THANKS

to all of our contributors who stand in solidarity for those still working on their victory over depression, anxiety, suicidal thoughts and other mental illnesses.

Harley Love	Penny Blackburn	Cleonna Moore
Denesha Smith	Devorah Bee	D'yann Elaine
Michelle Williams	Leila Tualla	Annie Galang
Maisha Walker	Helen Rosenau	Monica Jemison
Carole Cramer	Bree K. Jones	G.G. The Storyteller
Katherine Parker	Heather Pease	LaLa Deville
Rebecca Padilla	Janette Valenzo	Shaquan Lewis
Myah Rayne Mays	Cassandra Clark	Saturday & Lexi
Anna De La Cruz	Jennifer Furner	Cherish Hart
Mimi Lam	Risa Mykland	Ashlee Barcellos
Janaan.Dy	Emilee J. Grochowski	Renee "Kooki" Chatman
MarieJo L'Espérance	Brandi Mallory	Quitta Ineice
Lee Phillips	Sistar Outspoken	Nina13
Aubrey Eason	Blu & Ty'Lonnie	Queen Ex
Shelby Wills	Kelsey Bryan-Zwick	

WRITERS

MarieJo L'Espérance, "My Psoriatic Arthritis Gives the Toast at my 34th Birthday Party"

Shelby Wills, "Farewell"

Penny Blackburn, "It Is Too Late For Me To Be Young and Unashamed."

Devorah Bee, "Queen Bee of My Brain"

Heather Pease, "Journaling Through a Panic Attack" and "Keep Yourself Alive"

Jennifer Furner, "Letter to my Unborn Child"

Xylophone Mykland, "Bandaids"

Janaan Dy, "Her Escape", "Save Me", and "YOUR SUPER POWER"

PHOTO CRED

Dezi White

Tabitha "Tabs" Key